D1716921

CHANGING DESERT ENVIRONMENTS

LISA A. MCPARTLAND

PowerKiDS
press

New York

Published in 2020 by The Rosen Publishing Group, Inc.
29 East 21st Street, New York, NY 10010

First Edition

Editor: Jane Katirgis
Book Design: Reann Nye

Photo Credits: Series art Xiebiyun/Shutterstock.com; Alexander Tolstykh/Shutterstock.com; Cafe Racer/Shutterstock.com; cover Kenneth Keifer/Shutterstock.com; p. 4 Pearl-diver/Shutterstock.com; p. 5 yellow_cam/Shutterstock.com; p. 7 Jason Edwards/National Geographic/Getty Images; p. 8 Oleksandra Korobova/Moment/Getty Images; p. 9 Kayla Funk/Shutterstock.com; p. 10 alantobey/E+/Getty Images; p. 11 Anton Foltin/Shutterstock.com; p. 13 Homo Cosmicos/Shutterstock.com; p. 14 Paulo Miguel Costa/Shutterstock.com; p. 15 online express/Shutterstock.com; p. 16 Milosbeo/Shutterstock.com; p. 17 Craig P. Jewell/Moment/Getty Images; p. 18 Eric Isselee/Shutterstock.com; p. 19 2630ben/Shutterstock.com; p. 20 Calin Tatu/Shutterstock.com; p. 21 Ritesh Chaudhary/Shutterstock.com; p. 22 FloridaStock/Shutterstock.com; p. 23 Ungnoi Lookjeab/Shutterstock.com; p. 24 Sierralara/Shutterstock.com; p. 25 Daniel Prudek/Shutterstock.com; p. 26 seasoning_17/Shutterstock.com; p. 27 IrinaK/Shutterstock.com; p. 29 Alexxxey/Shutterstock.com; p. 30 Galyna Andrushko/Shutterstock.com.

Cataloging-in-Publication Data

Names: McPartland, Lisa A.
Title: Changing desert environments / Lisa A. McPartland.
Description: New York : PowerKids Press, 2020. | Series: Human impact on Earth: cause and effect | Includes glossary and index.
Identifiers: ISBN 9781725300200 (pbk.) | ISBN 9781725300224 (library bound) | ISBN 9781725300217 (6pack)
Subjects: LCSH: Deserts–Juvenile literature. | Desert ecology–Juvenile literature.
Classification: LCC GB612. M37 2020 | DDC 551.41'5–dc23

Manufactured in the United States of America

CPSIA Compliance Information: Batch #CSPK19. For Further Information contact Rosen Publishing, New York, New York at 1-800-237-9932.

CONTENTS

DESERT ENVIRONMENTS

Did you know that some penguins actually live in a desert? Did you know that deserts are found around the world and do not occur only in hot climates? People have had a great impact on how deserts have changed over time. However, people can make changes so this biome can thrive. A biome is a complex community with **distinctive** plants and animals that is maintained under the **climatic** conditions of a region.

This book will teach you about different types of deserts and about the plants and animals that live in each. This book will also discuss how people have impacted deserts and how we can reverse the negative impacts we have had on the biome.

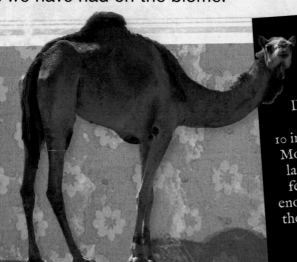

IMPACT FACTS

Deserts occur where rainfall is less than 10 inches (25 cm) each year. Most deserts do not have large mammals because few mammals can store enough water or withstand the extreme temperatures of these areas.

The Namaqua chameleon lives mainly in the sandy desert regions of the African country Namibia.

DESERT TYPES AND ANIMALS

There are four types of desert biomes. Deserts can be hot and dry, semiarid, coastal, or cold. Hot and dry deserts have seasons that are mostly warm, but they get very hot in the summer. Temperatures can be very hot during the day and very cold at night. This is because there is not much **humidity**, which would block heat from the sun. Temperatures can rise to 120°F (49°C) and fall to 0°F (−18°C)! Small mammals, insects, birds, reptiles, and **arachnids** live in these deserts. These animals look for food when it is cooler, such as at dusk, dawn, or night.

Semiarid deserts have long, dry summers. The winters see little rainfall. Temperatures range from 50°F (10°C) at night to 100°F (38°C) during the day. Animals that live in semiarid deserts include skunks, jackrabbits, and reptiles.

IMPACT FACTS

About one-fifth to one-third of Earth's surface is covered by deserts. Most people think of sand when they think of deserts. Most deserts are not covered by sand. Most deserts have rocky surfaces.

The Antarctic Polar Desert is the largest desert in the world and covers the continent of Antarctica.

THE LARGEST DESERTS

The two largest deserts might surprise you because they are not in hot climates. One, the Antarctic Polar Desert, covers Antarctica. The other, the Arctic Polar Desert, covers parts of Alaska, Canada, Greenland, Iceland, Norway, Sweden, Finland, and Russia. Each desert is more than 5 million square miles (13 million km²)! The largest nonpolar desert is the Sahara in Africa. It covers about 3.5 million square miles (9 million km²). To compare, the largest desert in North America, the Great Basin Desert, is 190,000 square miles (492,098 km²).

Coastal deserts are found where land meets the ocean. They have cool winters followed by long, warm summers. The low temperature is about 25°F (−4°C), and the high temperature is about 95°F (35°C). Insects, toads, reptiles, and even eagles live in these deserts.

IMPACT FACTS

Some penguins live on Antarctica, but not all penguins live there. The Humboldt penguin lives on the coasts of Chile and Peru.

Coyotes were originally plains animals. However, they are very good at adapting to other environments, such as deserts.

Cold deserts have long, cold winters with snowfall. The summers are short, wet, and warm. Rain also falls during the winter, and sometimes rain falls over the summer. Temperatures can be as cold as 28°F (−2°C) in the winter and as warm as 78°F (26°C) in the summer. Most animals in these deserts are **burrowers**. Some animals that live in these deserts include lizards, jackrabbits, coyotes, mice, penguins, and polar bears. Deer also can be found in the winter.

DESERT PLANTS

Besides having varied temperature ranges and animal life, each type of desert has different types of plants. Hot and dry deserts have shallow, rocky soil. Most plants are short, woody trees or shrubs that grow close to the ground.

IMPACT FACTS

When you think of desert plants, you probably think of cactus. While the cactus is mostly found in hot, dry places, some can be found in Alaska or near Antarctica.

A cactus and a brittlebush grow in an Arizona desert. Each type of desert has its own types of plants.

The soil in semiarid deserts is loose sand or gravel. Many plants there have spines or shiny leaves. The spines provide shade, and the shiny leaves reflect the sun's heat.

Coastal deserts have fine soil that can support plants with roots that are close to the surface. These roots soak up rainwater quickly. Plants in coastal deserts include bushes, grasses, and flowers.

In cold deserts, plants are found far apart. Most plants lose their leaves during the colder weather.

EARTH'S TILT LEADS TO CHANGES

Earth's position has impacted deserts. The planet tilts on its axis. This means Earth is tilted a certain degree toward the sun. Over time, the tilt changes as Earth wobbles like a spinning top. The changing degree of tilt causes changes in weather patterns. This could bring too much or too little rain to deserts. The tilt also affects the amount of sunlight reaching different parts of the world.

Some scientists believe that about 20,000 years ago, a change in Earth's tilt caused ice to melt in the polar deserts. This led to the end of the last ice age. An ice age is a period of global cooling with recurring **glacier** growth. Scientists also say that Earth's tilt changed about 8,000 years ago from 24.1 degrees to today's 23.5 degrees.

The Sahara in northern Africa is the third-largest desert in the world and the largest nonpolar desert. Some scientists believe that changes in Earth's tilt shaped the desert more than 5,000 years ago.

OTHER NATURAL CHANGES

Over time, nature has had many effects on **ecosystems** such as deserts. For example, animals searching for new homes have entered deserts to hunt for new food sources. This has caused there to be fewer of the plants or animals that are normally found in these deserts.

Weather patterns can change desert environments. Plants, such as this tree, might not be able to survive if too little rain falls.

Weather systems not related to Earth's tilt also can cause natural changes to deserts. Changing rain patterns could cause too much or too little rainfall. If too little rain falls, plants and animals might not be able to survive. If too much rain falls, this could cause land to **erode**. Other hazards—such as volcano eruptions, earthquakes, and diseases—also can harm the ecosystems of deserts. While natural changes have occurred slowly over time, people have changed Earth quickly and on a large scale.

15

HOW PEOPLE HAVE CHANGED DESERTS

Many human activities have changed deserts. People have built cities and highways in deserts. This has displaced animals and plants that are native to desert areas. People living in these desert cities have also brought vehicles with them, which has caused air pollution.

Fiber optic cables are a way to connect one urban area to another. When these cables pass through deserts, they disrupt the fragile ecosystems and allow weeds to grow. Other human activities can also harm deserts. **Irrigation** used to grow crops has caused high salt levels in the soil. The resulting high levels of salt have reduced the amount of plants available to consumers. Off-road vehicles can hurt desert habitats where desert plants and animals live. Also, humans have used deserts for nuclear weapons testing and nuclear waste dumping.

FIBER OPTIC CABLE

The Great Victoria Desert is Australia's largest desert. This desert is one of the least populated areas on Earth.

FROM FOREST TO DESERT

Millions of years ago, the Great Victoria Desert in Australia was a large rain forest. This desert has been mostly dry land for the past 100,000 years. Australia's Aboriginal people once called the desert home. Aboriginal people are those who are indigenous to the area, which means they lived there first. The harsh climate is one reason few people live in this desert now. Also, Australia's government forced people out of their desert homes so the desert could be used to test weapons.

People's use of **natural resources** also affects deserts. Humans find many resources in deserts, such as gold, silver, oil, natural gas, and diamonds. Digging resources out of the ground causes a lot of damage. Chemicals used in gold mining may poison animals. Oil and natural gas drilling may ruin desert habitats and pollute the land and water. Mines that are dug to find these resources leave open pits in the land. This makes it hard to return the land to its original state and hard to reuse the land.

Desert animals also are resources. Humans have hunted many animals in deserts. Many of those animals have become extinct, which means those animals no longer exist. Other animals have become endangered, which means they could become extinct.

The East African cheetah is in danger of becoming extinct.

ANIMALS DISAPPEARING

Many animals in the Sahara are endangered. They are in danger of no longer existing. Some endangered desert animals include antelopes, gazelles, lions, tortoises, and cheetahs. Some extinct animals from deserts around the world include the West African black rhinoceros, the Tecopa pupfish that once lived in the Mojave Desert, and the lesser bilby that once lived in Australia. Humans harm animals by using more land, hunting animals, and polluting the environment.

CLIMATE CHANGE

Climate change is affecting deserts. Climate change means there are changes in weather patterns across the planet. One large change is global warming. This is an increase in the average temperature of Earth's atmosphere. As Earth gets warmer, the heat causes the oceans to become warmer and more water to **evaporate**. This causes storms that have more energy.

Global warming also affects wind patterns. Changing wind patterns will impact the climate of deserts.

Many scientists have concluded that our dependence on fossil fuels, such as oil and natural gas, is a major cause of global warming.

POLAR BEARS IN DANGER

Polar bears live in the Arctic Polar Desert. There are about 26,000 polar bears on Earth. Climate change is leading to the melting of polar bear habitats. This means that polar bears have less snow and ice to make their homes. Seals also make their homes on polar ice. If there is less ice, there will be fewer seals for polar bears to hunt for food. Polar bears also face the threat of drowning if sea ice melts due to rising temperatures.

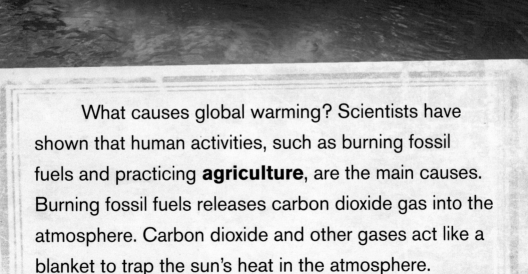

What causes global warming? Scientists have shown that human activities, such as burning fossil fuels and practicing **agriculture**, are the main causes. Burning fossil fuels releases carbon dioxide gas into the atmosphere. Carbon dioxide and other gases act like a blanket to trap the sun's heat in the atmosphere.

How is climate change affecting deserts? The Arctic and Antarctic deserts are changing because polar ice is melting. This leaves less land available for animals, such as polar bears and seals. The snow and glaciers in the polar deserts also provide freshwater to other parts of the world, including other deserts. When the snow and glaciers melt, there is less freshwater in other deserts. This will lead to less water for desert plants and animals.

Climate change could also bring floods or droughts to deserts. Plants and animals might not be able to survive these weather changes. **Prey** animals might be forced to move to cooler and wetter places. This would leave fewer food sources for **predator** animals that stay in the deserts.

Polar bears aren't the only creatures at risk from climage change. Many species around the world will be in danger.

THE GREENHOUSE EFFECT

The greenhouse effect describes the natural way Earth is warmed. The sun's energy enters the atmosphere. Some of the sun's energy is reflected back into space. However, some of the sun's energy is trapped in the atmosphere by greenhouse gases. Greenhouse gases include water vapor, carbon dioxide, methane, and ozone. Humans have polluted the atmosphere with too much carbon dioxide by burning fossil fuels to run cars, airplanes, and power plants. This has helped Earth trap more heat than it should. It causes global warming and climate change.

PROTECTING DESERTS

Deserts must be protected because they are home to many plants and animals. Government leaders are acting to protect deserts. For example, the California Desert Protection Act created the Mojave National Preserve to protect the Mojave Desert. The act limits mining and grazing in the desert.

Around the world, government leaders have agreed to address climate change to protect all biomes, including deserts. Governments signed the Paris Agreement and promised to reduce greenhouse gases that are polluting and overheating the atmosphere.

THE EXPANDING GOBI DESERT

Human activities are causing desertification in the greener lands around the Gobi Desert in China and Mongolia. Desertification means lands that are not deserts are becoming deserts. People and industries cause desertification by polluting the air, cutting down forests, and using up water supplies. Also, dust storms have increased. Dust storms often carry **toxins** such as heavy metals, viruses, and bacteria. Recently, China made changes to protect the rich farmland around the Gobi Desert. Changes included decreasing air pollution and using renewable resources, such as solar and wind power.

Today, about 27 percent of China has been desertified. This desertified area affects a population of 400 million people. To compare, that's more than the entire population of the United States, which has about 329 million people!

Environmental groups are also working to restore deserts. This means the groups are trying to return deserts to the natural states they were in before humans harmed deserts. These groups plant seeds so desert plants can grow. The groups also manage water and **rejuvenate** soil so plants can survive.

USING TECHNOLOGY

Technology is being used to protect desert biomes and life. One example involves the desert tortoise that lives in the Mojave Desert in California. People caused a large decline in the tortoise population. People brought off-road vehicles and diseases into the desert, which killed many tortoises. They also brought landfills, sewage ponds, and golf courses to the desert. These things attracted more ravens, a predatory bird, to the area. Ravens began to eat more baby tortoises.

IMPACT FACTS

In 2014, Hardshell Labs was created to protect desert tortoises. The company created 3-D fake baby tortoises and lasers to scare away ravens. These technologies do not hurt the ravens.

Hardshell Labs hopes to turn saving the desert tortoise into an activity similar to a video game. Players at home could remotely control rovers and lasers to help protect the tortoises from ravens and other predators.

To protect baby tortoises, scientists used 3-D printers to make fake baby tortoises. The scientists then put a natural chemical in the fake tortoises that ravens do not like. This kept the ravens away from the fake and real tortoises.

HOW CAN YOU HELP?

Are you wondering how you can help to protect deserts, even if you do not live near a desert? There are several things you can do. First, work to reduce your carbon footprint. A carbon footprint is how much carbon dioxide each person is responsible for putting into the atmosphere. You could ask your parents to drive or fly in airplanes less often. You could walk or use a bicycle for shorter trips. You also could recycle. Instead of buying something new, try to fix what you have or use it until it no longer can be used. This makes less waste.

Community groups also work to protect deserts. You could collect money and donate to one of these groups. If you hope to make a larger impact, you could write a letter to your local congressperson, the Environmental Protection Agency, or even the president of the United States!

There are many things you can do to help protect deserts, such as writing to government leaders who have the power to make big changes. >

REVIVING DESERTS

Peter Westerveld was born in the African country of Tanzania. When he was young, he saw the effects of climate change and drought. As an adult, he worked to help stop desertification by creating the Westerveld Conservation Trust. One of his inventions was called contour trenching. In contour trenching, deep trenches are dug. These trenches hold rainwater so the water does not quickly run off hills or evaporate. Contour trenching also helps to stop soil from eroding.

WHAT'S NEXT?

People have had a great impact on deserts. Mining, overgrazing, and polluting the environment are ways that humans have caused harm to deserts. These activities have also caused desert animals to become endangered or extinct. The need for fossil fuels has led to climate change, which has also negatively affected deserts.

People can make changes so that deserts can thrive. Each person can play a role in decreasing the amount of waste that is put into the air, into the water, and onto the land in this biome. People also should respect deserts by making sure human activities do not hurt the plants and animals that make deserts their home. We all can play a role in protecting deserts.

GLOSSARY

agriculture: The science or occupation of producing crops or raising livestock.

arachnid: Any of a class of arthropods, such as a spider, that has a segmented body divided into two regions, eight legs, and no antennae.

burrower: An animal that digs a hole in the ground for shelter or protection.

climatic: Of or related to a region with specified weather conditions.

distinctive: Clearly marking a person or a thing as different from others.

ecosystem: Systems of living and nonliving things—such as animals, plants, and water—interacting with their environments.

erode: To wear away.

evaporate: To remove some water, as by heating.

glacier: A large body of ice moving slowly down slopes or valleys or spreading outward on land surfaces.

humidity: The amount of moisture in the air.

irrigation: The supply of water through artificial, or human-made, means.

natural resource: Something found in nature that is valuable to humans.

predator: An animal that hunts other animals for food.

prey: An animal hunted by other animals for food.

rejuvenate: To give new vigor, or energy, to something.

toxin: A substance that is very poisonous to living things.

INDEX

WEBSITES

Due to the changing nature of Internet links, PowerKids Press has developed an
online list of websites related to the subject of this book. This site is updated regularly.
Please use this link to access the list: www.powerkidslinks.com/HIOE/desert